W9-BYX-893

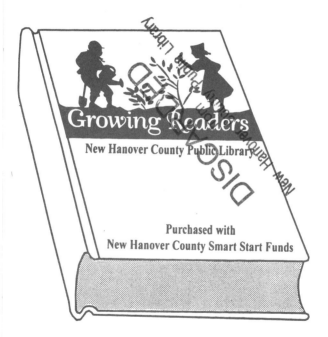

Growing Readers

New Hanover County Public Library

Purchased with
New Hanover County Smart Start Funds

The Grain Group

by Helen Frost

Consulting Editor: Gail Saunders-Smith, Ph.D.
Consultant: Linda Hathaway
Health Educator
McMillen Center for Health Education

Pebble Books

an imprint of Capstone Press
Mankato, Minnesota

NEW HANOVER COUNTY
PUBLIC LIBRARY
201 CHESTNUT STREET
WILMINGTON, NC 28401

Pebble Books are published by Capstone Press
151 Good Counsel Drive, P.O. Box 669, Mankato, Minnesota 56002
http://www.capstone-press.com

Copyright © 2000 Capstone Press. All rights reserved.
No part of this book may be reproduced without written permission
from the publisher. The publisher takes no responsibility for the use of any
of the materials or methods described in this book, nor for the products thereof.
Printed in the United States of America.

1 2 3 4 5 6 05 04 03 02 01 00

Library of Congress Cataloging-in-Publication Data
Frost, Helen, 1949–
    The grain group/by Helen Frost.
    p. cm.—(Food guide pyramid)
    Includes bibliographical references and index.
    Summary: Simple text and photographs present the foods that are part of the
grain group and their nutritional importance.
    ISBN 0-7368-0538-9
    1. Nutrition—Juvenile literature. 2. Grain—Juvenile literature. [1. Grain.
2. Nutrition.] I. Title. II. Series.
TX355 .F77   2000
613.2—dc21
                                       99-047741

Note to Parents and Teachers

The Food Guide Pyramid series supports national science standards related to physical health and nutrition. This book describes and illustrates the grain group. The photographs support early readers in understanding the text. The repetition of words and phrases helps early readers learn new words. This book also introduces early readers to subject-specific vocabulary words, which are defined in the Words to Know section. Early readers may need assistance to read some words and to use the Table of Contents, Words to Know, Read More, Internet Sites, and Index/Word List sections of the book.

Table of Contents

The food guide pyramid shows the foods you need to stay healthy. The grain group is at the bottom of the food guide pyramid.

Grains are seeds from cereal plants such as wheat, rice, and corn. Foods made from these seeds are in the grain group.

Bread is in
the grain group.

Breakfast cereal is in the grain group.

Popcorn is in
the grain group.

Rice is in
the grain group.

Crackers are in
the grain group.

18

Pasta is in
the grain group.

You need 6 to 11 servings from the grain group every day. Food from the grain group gives you energy that lasts a long time.

Words to Know

energy—the strength to be active without becoming tired; foods in the grain group give you energy that lasts a long time.

food guide pyramid—a triangle split into six areas to show the different foods people need; a pyramid is big at the bottom and small at the top; people need more food from the bottom of the food guide pyramid than from the top.

grain—the seed of a cereal plant such as wheat, rice, corn, or barley

healthy—fit and well; following the food guide pyramid helps keep you healthy.

serving—a helping of food or drink; one serving from the grain group is one slice of bread, one ounce (30 grams) of ready-to-eat breakfast cereal, 1/2 cup (125 ml) of cooked cereal or rice, or 1/2 cup (125 ml) of pasta.

Read More

Frost, Helen. *Eating Right.* The Food Guide Pyramid. Mankato, Minn.: Pebble Books, 2000.

Kalbacken, Joan. *The Food Pyramid.* A True Book. New York: Children's Press, 1998.

McGinty, Alice B. *Staying Healthy: Eating Right.* The Library of Healthy Living. New York: PowerKids Press, 1997.

Powell, Jillian. *Rice.* Everyone Eats. Austin, Texas: Raintree Steck-Vaughn, 1997.

Internet Sites

Food Guide Pyramid
http://www.kidshealth.org/kid/food/pyramid.html

Food Guide Pyramid Game
http://www.nppc.org/cgi-bin/pyramid

Kids Food Cyberclub
http://www.kidsfood.org//kf_cyber.html

Nutrition Cafe
http://exhibits.pacsci.org/nutrition

Index/Word List

Word Count: 108
Early-Intervention Level: 10

Editorial Credits
Mari C. Schuh, editor; Heather Kindseth, cover designer; Sara A. Sinnard, illustrator;
    Kia Bielke, illustrator; Kimberly Danger, photo researcher

Photo Credits
David F. Clobes, 1
Gary Randall/FPG International LLC, cover
Gregg R. Andersen, 6
Jim Cummins/FPG International LLC, 20
Kim Stanton, 16
Photo Agora, 12
Photo Network/Vic Bider, 8; Esbin-Anderson, 10
Unicorn Stock Photos/Jim Shippee, 14; Steve Bourgeois, 18

Growing Readers
New Hanover County
Public Library
201 Chestnut Street
Wilmington, NC 28401